Healing
Spells and
Magic

Beatrice Aurelia Crowley

Erebus Society

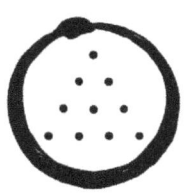

Erebus Society

All rights reserved; no part of this publication may be reproduced or transmitted by any means, electronic, mechanical, photocopying or otherwise, without the prior written permission of the publisher except for the use of brief quotations in a book review.

First published in Great Britain in 2025
Erebus Society

First Edition

Copyright © Beatrice Aurelia Crowley 2025
Book Design Copyright © Erebus Society 2025
Cover Copyright © Ars Corvinus 2025

ISBN: 978-1-912461-66-0

www.ErebusSociety.com

Table of Contens

What is Healing Magic? 1
Magical Correspondences 5
Important Herbs to Mention 13

Spells 15

Absent Healing Spell 16
All-Purpose Healing Spell 17
Ancient Folk Ant Healing 18
Apollo's Healing 19
Banishing Sickness from Yourself 22
Bubble Healing 23
Cloth and Ribbon Healing Charm 26
Cloth Healing Charm 28
Cold Fire - Healing Fevers 29
Colds and Flu Ease and Hasten 30
Compassionate Healing 31
Cord and Tree 32
Divine Water Meditation 34
Elemental Healing Ritual 36
Enchanted Crystal Healing 38
Enchanted Poppet Healing 40
Empowering Healing Remedy 42
Eucalyptus Healing Spell 43
Flaming Image Healing 44
Gaia's Healing 46
Heal a Friend or Relative 48
Heal All 49
Healing Bath Meditation 50
Healing Circle of Fire 51
Healing of the Seven Candles 52
Healing Ritual 54
Hematite Healing 55
No Ingredients Healing Chant 56
Protect and Maintain Good Health 57
Protect Against Disease 58
Salt Burial to Heal Another Person 60

Shower Waterfall of Healing 61
Silver Moon Healing Charm 62
Stream healing Ritual 64

Concoctions.. 65

Balm of Gilead Salve 66
Bath Water 68
Healing Honey Remedies 69
Daily Health 69
Honey Flu Remedy 70
Honey Throat Syrup 70
Garlic and Honey Wound Dressing 71
Healing Oil 72
Healing Potpourri I 74
Healing Potpourri II 75
Healing Potpourri III 76
Healing Tea 77
Irish Healing Water 78
Jewelweed Salve 80
Menopause Elixir 82
Muscle Pain Reliever 84
Moon Water Tonic 86
Rejuvenating Bath 87
Pain Reliever Salve 88
Soothing Bath 90

What is Healing Magic?

INTRODUCTION

Healing magic is a deeply compassionate form of spellcraft that transcends the simple repair of physical injuries to encompass the restoration of spirit, mind, and body. It is the art of rejuvenation, a sacred energy flow that aims to restore equilibrium, alleviate pain, and revive vitality in oneself and others. Healing magic, whether achieved through touch, incantation, or the use of herbs and crystals, exemplifies the conviction that life is interlaced with divine energy, which can be cultivated, restored, and fortified.

This magic serves as a conduit between terrestrial life and the invisible powers of healing, encompassing the calming essence of sacred waters and the luminous energy invoked by spells. It synchronises the healer with the universe's natural cycles, enabling the channelling of energies that foster wholeness, harmony, and resilience.

What, in essence, constitutes healing magic? In what ways does it appear across various traditions, and what significance does it hold in the overarching framework of the esoteric? Let us examine this revered art, its origins, techniques, and lasting influence in the practices of witches, shamans, and mystics.

UNDERSTANDING HEALING MAGIC

Healing magic encompasses not only bodily repair but also mental, emotional, and spiritual well-being. It is an act of benevolent sorcery, motivated by intention, energy, and profound comprehension of equilibrium. Healing magic operates based on several fundamental principles:

1. Restoration - Reinstating an individual or environment to its inherent condition of health and equilibrium.

2. Cleansing and Release — Eliminating emotional trauma, energetic obstructions, or spiritual injuries.

3. Rejuvenation - Augmenting vitality, vigour, and resistance via mystical intervention.

Healing magic can be executed for oneself, others, animals, plants, and environments impacted by negative energy.

METHODS OF HEALING MAGIC

Herbal Healing and Potions - The efficacy of botanical remedies is one of the most ancient and potent modalities of healing magic. Herbs including lavender, chamomile, rosemary, and echinacea are incorporated into drinks, tinctures, or baths to facilitate recovery.

Energy Healing and Laying of Hands — The transmission of universal life force energy (chi, prana, or Reiki) for healing via direct contact or aura manipulation.

Crystal Healing - Crystals like amethyst, clear quartz, rose quartz, and bloodstone are employed to enhance healing energy, eliminate obstructions, and restore equilibrium.

Candle Healing Magic - Distinct candle hues are employed for various facets of healing:

1. Blue – Emotional restoration and serenity
2. Green – Physical recovery and revitalisation
3. White – Spiritual purification and regeneration

Water and Moon Healing — Ritual baths, consecrated water, and moon-infused elixirs are employed to purify the body and spirit.

Chants & Sound Healing - Vibrational energy is employed through chants, singing bowls, bells, and drumming to alleviate disease and restore energetic equilibrium.

Dream and Sleep Magic - Employing spells and charms to promote profound slumber, prophetic dreams, and subconscious healing.

Origins and History of Healing Magic

Healing magic has been practiced for millennia, intertwined into the traditions of ancient civilisations, religious rites, folk medicines, and spiritual ceremonies. Across cultures, healers have been respected as custodians of wisdom, attuned to the rhythms of life and the divine energies that regulate wellness and vitality.

Ancient Civilisations and Sacred Healers

In Ancient Egypt, priests and priestesses invoked Heka (divine magic) to restore health. The temples of Isis and Sekhmet served as healing centres, utilising sacred oils, incantations, and herbal remedies to address ailments. Amulets and charms, including the Eye of Horus, were utilised to prevent illness and enhance vitality.

In Mesopotamia, the Babylonians and Sumerians invoked Ea (Enki), the deity of wisdom and healing, through clay tablets inscribed with prayers, symbols, and medicinal incantations. These texts, frequently integrated with herbal tonics and ritual purification, constituted one of the earliest documented medical systems.

In Ancient Greece and Rome, the Greeks perceived healing as a divine endowment, harnessing the influence of Asclepius, the deity of medicine. Asclepions, or healing temples, served as venues for the sick to engage in rituals of incubation, purification, and herbal therapy. The Romans enhanced these practices by integrating ritual baths, planetary alignments, and divine offerings to promote health restoration.

Celtic, Norse, and Indigenous Traditions

Celtic Healing Magic – Druids and priestesses collaborated intimately with nature, utilising sacred wells, lunar blessings, and medicinal herbs to remedy ailments. The goddess Brigid, esteemed for her dominion over healing, poetry, and midwifery, was frequently invoked during periods of illness.

Norse Healing Practices - The Norse employed runes and seidr magic to summon healing forces. Rune spells, especially those inscribed on wood or bone, were thought to transmit divine power to the affected individual. The goddess Eir, a divine healer, was venerated in restoration rites.

Indigenous Healing Practices — Numerous Native American, African, and Polynesian traditions prioritise healing magic as central to spiritual practice. Shamans, healers, and spiritual leaders utilised spirit guides, herbal remedies, energy practices, and drumming rituals to restore harmony between the body and spirit.

Medieval and Renaissance Healing Magic

Folk Healers and Cunning Folk — In mediaeval Europe, wise women, cunning men, and herbalists maintained the ancient wisdom of phytotherapy and energy healing. Numerous individuals were charged with witchcraft, despite their techniques being fundamentally based on ancestral knowledge and natural treatments.

Christianity and Alchemical Healing - The emergence of Christianity frequently associated healing magic with saints, sacred relics, and prayers. Simultaneously, alchemists pursued the "Elixir of Life," conducting experiments with herbal concoctions, metals, and celestial alignments to extend longevity.

Magical Correspondences

Herbs

These herbs and crystals serve as potent companions in healing magic, applicable for physical restoration, emotional well-being, or spiritual rebirth. They may be utilised in rituals, baths, teas, crystal grids, or meditation activities to facilitate healing in all dimensions of life.

Aloe Vera

A sacred herb for soothing, regeneration, and physical healing, particularly for burns, skin issues, and wounds.

Angelica

A powerful herb of protection and divine healing, used to ward off illness and promote spiritual well-being.

Basil

Known for its calming and anti-inflammatory properties, basil is used in healing teas and baths to restore balance and vitality.

Calendula (Marigold)

A potent herb for skin healing, purification, and reducing inflammation, commonly used in salves and washes.

Chamomile

A gentle but effective herb for emotional healing, relaxation, and easing anxiety, often used in teas and dream magic.

Comfrey

A powerful herb for bone, muscle, and tissue healing, traditionally used in poultices and salves.

Echinacea

A well-known immune booster, used to ward off illness, speed recovery, and cleanse the body of toxins.

Elderflower

A sacred herb of renewal and purification, often used in healing teas and rituals for longevity and immune strength.

Fennel

Known for its digestive healing properties, fennel is used to soothe stomach ailments and aid in energetic detoxification.

Garlic

A potent antibacterial and antifungal herb, traditionally used for protection and healing infections.

Ginger

A warming and restorative herb, used to boost circulation, ease pain, and aid in healing fevers and colds.

Hawthorn

Sacred to heart healing and emotional balance, this herb is used to strengthen love, courage, and heart health.

Holy Basil (Tulsi)

A revered spiritual and physical healer, known for its immune-boosting and stress-relieving properties.

Lavender

A universal calming and healing herb, used to ease stress, headaches, and sleep disturbances.

Lemon Balm

A gentle but powerful herb for calming the nervous system, reducing anxiety, and promoting emotional healing.

Mugwort

Used in dream magic and deep spiritual healing, helping with psychic balance and trauma release.

Peppermint

A cooling herb that aids digestion, clears headaches, and revitalises energy, used in healing teas and baths.

Rose

A sacred herb for emotional healing and heart chakra work, used in teas, baths, and anointing oils for self-love and grief healing.

Rosemary

A deeply restorative herb, used to cleanse energy, promote mental clarity, and aid in memory healing.

Yarrow

A sacred wound healer and energy balancer, traditionally used to stop bleeding, cleanse the aura, and strengthen resilience.

CRYSTALS AND MINERALS

Crystals and minerals are primordial protectors, originating from the earth's core and infused with potent vibrations. They function as channels of energy, enhancing intention and providing protection against harm. The following is a brief compilation of their names, properties, and their associations for protection:

AMETHYST

A master spiritual healer, used to calm the mind, ease anxiety, and aid emotional balance.

AQUAMARINE

A stone of emotional healing and purification, helping to soothe grief and promote inner peace.

BLACK TOURMALINE

A powerful grounding and protective stone, used to absorb negative energy and promote physical resilience.

BLOODSTONE

A stone of physical strength and endurance, known for cleansing the blood and supporting immune health.

BLUE LACE AGATE

A gentle healer for the throat chakra, helping to ease stress, promote clear communication, and reduce tension.

Carnelian

A stone of vitality and life force, used to stimulate healing energy, boost circulation, and restore strength.

Celestite

A celestial stone that brings divine healing energy, particularly for emotional and spiritual wounds.

Chrysoprase

A heart-centered healing stone that helps release trauma and promotes emotional renewal.

Clear Quartz

Known as the "Master Healer", this crystal amplifies healing energy, purifies the aura, and restores balance.

Fluorite (Green or Purple)

A cleansing crystal that removes energetic blockages and promotes healing on all levels.

Garnet

A stone of strength and regeneration, used to stimulate healing, improve circulation, and boost recovery.

Green Aventurine

A heart-healing stone that brings renewal, growth, and physical vitality.

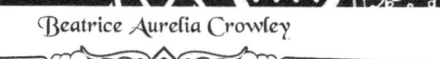

Hematite

A powerful grounding stone that absorbs negative energy and supports physical healing.

Jade (Green or White)

A revered stone for long life, emotional balance, and overall healing.

Lapis Lazuli

A deep spiritual healer, used to soothe emotional wounds and enhance intuition in healing work.

Malachite

A transformative healing stone that draws out trauma, supports emotional release, and strengthens resilience.

Moonstone

A gentle stone for feminine healing, hormone balance, and emotional stability.

Obsidian (Snowflake or Black)

A powerful psychic healer, helping to remove negative attachments and release past pain.

Rose Quartz

A sacred heart healer, promoting self-love, emotional harmony, and recovery from heartbreak or grief.

Selenite

A high-vibrational stone that clears stagnant energy, promotes spiritual healing, and restores clarity.

Important Herbs to Mention

Garlic:

Harness the power of garlic to lower blood pressure and cholesterol, and wield it as a potent antiseptic, antibiotic, and anticancer agent. It protects liver and brain cells with its medicinal properties. Add fresh garlic to your daily meals to invite health and protection into your life.

Ginger:

In ancient China and India, ginger was revered for its ability to tone, uplift, and warm the system. It stimulates digestion, enhances circulation, soothes upset stomachs, and alleviates nausea, aches, and pains. Consume ginger in candied slices, honey-based syrups, or as a comforting tea.

Green Tea:

Green tea, the cherished beverage of Japan, guards against heart disease and cancer. Offering a gentle form of caffeine, it serves as a powerful tonic for overall well-being. Replace your coffee, black tea, or cola with green tea for a healthy boost.

Milk Thistle:

An old European folk remedy, milk thistle detoxifies and enhances liver function. Ideal for those who consume alcohol, pharmaceuticals, or recreational drugs, and those exposed to toxins. Regular intake of this herb ensures your liver remains protected and vital.

Astragalus:

A popular Chinese herb, astragalus treats colds, flu, and chronic infections like bronchitis, sinusitis, and AIDS. It restores immunity, boosts vitality, and increases resistance to disease. Take astragalus capsules when you lack energy or feel stressed to restore your inner strength.

Ginseng:

Primarily recommended for men, ginseng stimulates and energizes, enhances sexual vitality, improves appetite, aids digestion, tones the skin and muscles, and balances hormones in women. It's a rejuvenator for the tired, elderly, and chronically ill. Enjoy ginseng in candies, teas, wines, or elixirs for its revitalizing magic.

Dong Quai:

Predominantly used by women, this Chinese herb builds blood, increases circulation, and regulates menstrual and reproductive disorders. Restore balance with dong quai in tincture or capsule form, inviting harmony and health into your body.

Maitake Mushrooms: Highly esteemed for their healing properties, maitake mushrooms protect against cancer, AIDS, chronic fatigue, hepatitis, allergies, and environmental illness. Incorporate maitake tablets or capsules into your diet to fortify your body against these ailments.

Spells

The Essential Book of Healing Spells and Magic

Absent Healing Spell
(FOR SOMEONE ELSE)

REQUIREMENTS:

✸ A picture of the patient
✸ A blue or green candle
✸ Sandalwood oil
✸ Clear quartz gemstone/crystal

INSTRUCTIONS:

Create a Protective Shield by projecting a white light shield around yourself to protect against the illness you are dealing with.

Hold the candle in your hands and project healing and love energy into it. Do the same with the clear quartz gemstone in order to charge them.

Anoint the candle with sandalwood oil, starting from the bottom and working up to the top, moving away from you. Visualize the illness leaving the person or imagine them surrounded by green healing energy.

Place the picture of the patient under the candle and light it. Then, place the clear quartz gemstone on top of the picture.

Chant the following words as the candle burns, visualizing the patient being healed:

> *Absent friend in need of care,*
> *Healing light now fills the air.*
> *By the flame and crystal's might,*
> *Health returns, pure and bright.*

Allow the candle to burn for at least 20 minutes. Light the candle once a day until the illness has subsided.

Once the healing is complete, bury the candle off your property and thoroughly cleanse the crystal.

Beatrice Aurelia Crowley

All-Purpose Healing Spell

REQUIREMENTS:

✻ 1 piece of amber or amethyst
✻ A green candle
✻ A piece of paper
✻ A pencil

INSTRUCTIONS:

Cast the circle, inviting the God, the Goddess, and the elements to join you.

On the piece of paper, write down the problem, describing the illness or injury you wish to heal.

Light the green candle, focusing on its healing light.

Lay down on the floor in the center of your circle and place the gemstone at the site of illness (e.g., on your throat if it is sore).

Close your eyes and imagine the illness or injury being drawn out and absorbed into the gemstone. Take your time with this process.

As you visualize the healing, chant the following:
"Stone of healing, draw out pain,
Illness fade, health remain.
By the candle's light and gemstone's might,
Restore me now, this sacred night."

When you feel the energy has transferred, burn the piece of paper in the candle's flame.

Thank the God, the Goddess, and the elements for their assistance.

Close the circle, sealing the energy.

Take the gemstone and the ashes from the paper outside and bury them in the ground, symbolizing the return of the illness to the earth.

Ancient Folk Ant Healing

REQUIREMENTS:

✼ A fresh hen's egg
✼ A small pot of your own urine
✼ An anthill in a natural setting

INSTRUCTIONS:

At dawn, collect your own urine in a small pot. With gratitude, acknowledge the body's natural processes and their connection to the earth.

Gently place the hen's egg in the pot of urine and bring it to a boil. As the liquid simmers, envision the egg absorbing the illness or negativity within you.

Once the egg is fully boiled, take it to a nearby anthill. With respect to nature's tiny workers, carefully bury the egg at the base of the anthill. Whisper the following incantation:

> "Ants of the earth, small and wise,
> As you consume, the sickness dies.
> Take this ailment far from me,
> Banish it to the earth, and set me free."

Walk away without looking back, trusting the ants to carry away your illness as they consume the egg. Feel the weight of your ailment lifting, and embrace the healing power of the natural world.

Apollo's Healing

REQUIREMENTS:

✤ White candle
✤ Piece of paper
✤ Ink pen
✤ Quartz crystal
✤ Mortar (or another cauldron-like object)
✤ Healing oil (Frankincense recommended)

INSTRUCTIONS:

Place the white candle, piece of paper, ink pen, quartz crystal, cauldron substitute (e.g., mortar), and healing oil on your altar.

Cast a Circle. Begin at the east. Visualize a pentacle of blue fire at each cardinal point:

East: Feel the wind across an open plain.

South: Absorb the warmth of the sun.

West: Stand atop a cliff overlooking a vast ocean.

North: Imagine great mountains cloaked in dark forests.

At the altar, clear your mind and set your intention to heal. Light the candle, saying:

"I dedicate this candle to thee, Lord Apollo the Physician, and ask your aid in fighting this illness."

Find a word that represents the illness (e.g., "meningitis" or "misery").

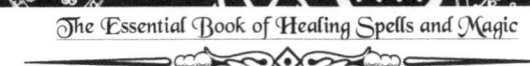

Write the word on the paper, saying:

"I imbue thee, paper, with the essence of this illness – thou shalt represent it for me in this ritual."

Douse the paper with the healing oil, saying:

"With this oil, I prepare thee."

Carefully hold the paper to the flame and let it catch fire. Drop it into the cauldron, chanting:

"With fire, I vanquish thee, [illness], in the name of Apollo the Physician I destroy thee."

Repeat this phrase three times.

Center yourself and hold the quartz crystal to your third eye. Breathe deeply, allowing the energy of the ritual to flow through the crystal.

For self-healing, absorb the energy from the crystal. For healing another, send the energy along a shining path to them.

Thank Apollo for his presence:

"I thank thee, Lord Apollo, for your presence here tonight – farewell, Lord!"

Close the circle by thanking each direction, starting from the north and ending at the east.

Ground the energy by reciting:

"Circle open but unbroken, power down to the ground."

Pound your staff or stamp three times to release the energy back into the earth.

You may leave the candle burning as a sign of ongoing healing, perhaps until you see improvement in the condition.

NOTES

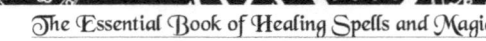

Banishing Sickness from Yourself

REQUIREMENTS:

✷ Athame, wand, or your index finger

INSTRUCTIONS:

Take your Athame, wand, or use your index finger. Draw a banishing pentagram in the air while chanting:

O sickness, vanish into the skies,
Pain, ascend where the clouds do rise,
Inflamed mist, fly through the air,
Let the breeze take you far from here,
Let the tempest chase you to distant lands,
Return to where you did no harm.

Feel the sickness lifting from your body, carried away by the winds.

NOTES

Bubble Healing
(CONTEMPORARY)

Requirements:

- Five small bowls
- Incense (spearmint and allspice on charcoal)
- Bubbles and bubble wand
- Food coloring: green, blue, red, yellow
- Picture of the sick person or their presence

Instructions:

Mix each color of food coloring (green, blue, red, yellow) with portions of the bubble solution in separate bowls.

In the fifth bowl, combine a small portion of each color with the bubble solution.

Cleanse your sacred area, cast the circle, call the Quarters, and invoke the God and the Goddess.

Light the incense, letting its scent fill the air.

Meditate on the purpose of the bubbles and healing. Visualize each bowl glowing with a white healing light.

Perform the following Healing Chants:

Fire Healing

Blow the red bubbles and chant three times:

"Fire above and fire below,
Take this pain, make it go.
Burn away, cleanse the soul,
Heal the body, make it whole."

Water Healing

Blow the blue bubbles and chant three times:

> "Water above and water below,
> Wash away pain, let it flow.
> Cleanse the form, pure and bright,
> Heal this soul, restore the light."

Air Healing

Blow the yellow bubbles and chant three times:

> "Air above and air below,
> Carry away pain, let it go.
> Enclose it within, let it be,
> Dry the body, soul set free."

Earth Healing

Blow the green bubbles and chant three times:

> "Earth around and earth below,
> Bury this pain, deep and slow.
> Hide it away, far from sight,
> Heal this life, day and night."

Unified Healing

Blow the bubbles from the mixed solution and chant three times:

> "In these bubbles, power resides,
> Healing corners, troubles hide.
> No more pain, ailments flee,
> Health and joy, blessed be."

Thank the Goddess and the God.

Release the Quarters.

Close the Circle.

NOTES

Cloth and Ribbon Healing Charm

REQUIREMENTS:

- A piece of soft cotton
- A length of red ribbon
- A white candle
- A small bowl of water infused with healing herbs (such as lavender or chamomile)

INSTRUCTIONS:

Light the white candle and place it on your altar.

Sit quietly and focus your intention on healing.

Take the piece of cotton and gently wrap it around your hand or the hand of the person in need of healing.

Bind the cotton with the red ribbon, securing it with a gentle knot.

Holding the hand wrapped in cotton, speak these words with intent:

> "Wrapped in cotton, bound with love,
> Protection from pain, like a glove.
> May the brightest blessings light,
> Surround thee now, this healing night."

Dip your fingers into the bowl of herb-infused water and sprinkle it lightly over the bound cotton, saying:

> "With water's touch, the pain departs,
> Healing flows and mends the heart.
> Spirits of light, gather near,
> Bless this soul, bring comfort here."

Let the candle burn for a while, visualizing the person being enveloped in a warm, healing glow.

Extinguish the candle and keep the cotton wrap on until you feel the healing process has begun.

NOTES

Cloth Healing Charm

REQUIREMENTS:

❀ A quiet space for concentration
❀ A white candle
❀ A piece of cotton cloth

INSTRUCTIONS:

Find a peaceful area where you can focus without interruptions. Light the white candle to represent purity and healing.

Close your eyes and think deeply of the person you wish to heal. Visualize them surrounded by a warm, glowing light, gradually getting better and regaining their strength.

Hold the piece of cotton cloth in your hands, infusing it with your loving energy. Chant the following words three times with intention and focus:

"Wrap thee in cotton, bind thee with love,
Protection from pain surrounds like a glove.
Brightest of blessings, surrounding thee this night,
For thou art cared for, healing thoughts take flight."

Keep the cotton cloth in a safe place or send it to the person you are healing, allowing the energy to continue its work.

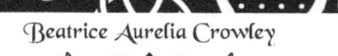

Beatrice Aurelia Crowley

Cold Fire - Healing Fevers

INSTRUCTIONS:

Begin by chanting the ancient Cornish invocation to St. Brigit to call upon the forces needed to heal:

> "Three maidens from the East did tread,
> One bore fire, two brought frost instead,
> Fire depart, let frost embed."

Stand or sit quietly, and visualize a powerful energy within you, like a cold, soothing fire.

Direct this energy into your hands, feeling them grow cool and vibrant with healing power.

Gently place your hands on the person's neck or forehead.

Envision the cold fire flowing from your hands into their body, seeking out and confronting the fever.

As you feel the fever's heat, set up a second channel in your mind to draw it away into your own body, but do not worry, you will not retain it.

Continue this until you sense the cold fire has subdued the fever's heat.

If the person shivers with fever, direct the excess heat to their skin while you combat the fever within. Embrace them if necessary to share warmth.

This method supplements traditional fever-reducers like aspirin and should be used while waiting for the medicine to take effect.

You might feel a slight warmth or flush, but rest assured, the fever will not transfer to you.

Repeat the spell as needed, particularly when the fever spikes, until the illness subsides.

Colds and Flu Ease and Hasten

REQUIREMENTS:

❀ 6 small green candles
❀ Matches
❀ Picture of sick friend (optional, visualization will suffice)

INSTRUCTIONS:

On the first day of symptoms, find a private space where you won't be disturbed. Gather your six green candles and matches. If you have a picture of your sick friend, keep it nearby. Otherwise, prepare to visualize their face clearly.

Sit comfortably and meditate over the candles, focusing your intention on healing your friend. Visualize them in perfect health, free from illness.

For six consecutive hours, light one candle each hour. As you light each candle, chant the following incantation three times while visualizing your friend's face or looking at their photo:

> Green candle and golden flame,
> Gather power in healing's name,
> Bring forth light to mend and heal,
> Focus on my friend's ordeal.
> When six hours pass, a quarter day,
> Take [Name]'s sickness far away.

Continue this process until all six candles have burned. After the sixth hour, let the healing energies work overnight. Your friend's symptoms should start to fade, either partially or completely, by morning.

Compassionate Healing

REQUIREMENTS:

✿ Human-shaped candle (appropriate gender)
✿ Myrrh or mint oil
✿ Photograph of the sick person

INSTRUCTIONS:

Write the name of the person you wish to heal on the candle.

Anoint the candle with myrrh or mint oil. As you do so, visualize healing energy as white light flowing from your fingers into the candle.

While anointing, recite:

*In the divine name of the Goddess who breathes life into us all,
I consecrate and charge this candle as a magical tool for healing.
Place the charged candle on top of a photograph of the sick person.
Light the wick of the candle. As it burns, concentrate on the person, willing them to be healthy and strong.*

Chant the following incantation as the candle burns:

*Magic mend and candle burn,
Sickness end; good health return.
Allow the candle to burn down completely.
Visualize the person recovering and regaining their strength.*

Cord and Tree

REQUIREMENTS:

❧ A red cord
❧ A strong, healthy tree with flexible branches
❧ An offering (e.g., fruit, herbs, or a token of gratitude)

INSTRUCTIONS:

As night approaches, gently tie a red cord around the neck of the person in need of healing.

At dawn, untie the red cord from the person immediately.

Re-tie the cord around a tree trunk or branch, transferring the illness to the tree, allowing it to disperse into the earth.

Leave an offering of gratitude at the base of the tree as thanks for its help in dispersing the illness.

Find a robust and healthy tree with flexible branches.

When you feel unwell, approach the tree and gently tie a knot in one of its branches, taking care not to harm the tree.

As you tie the knot, pour the illness into the knot, visualizing it leaving your body and entering the tree.

Spend several minutes focusing on transferring the disease into the knot.

Carefully untie the knot, visualizing the illness being released and absorbed into the earth.

Bury an offering at the base of the tree to complete the ritual and show your gratitude.

Chant:

*"With this red cord, illness bind,
In morning light, to tree assigned.
Tree so strong, branches bend,
Illness to earth, now descend.
Knot of healing, sickness flee,
Gratitude I offer unto thee."*

NOTES

Divine Water Meditation

REQUIREMENTS:

❃ 2 bowls of warm water
❃ A quiet space with access to bare earth or a comfortable floor

INSTRUCTIONS:

Begin by blessing or empowering the water in each bowl as you see fit. Pray to the God and Goddess, asking them to aid in your healing. Channel as much personal energy as you can into the water.

Lie upon the bare earth. If this is not possible, lying on the floor is acceptable. Stretch your arms out to the sides, placing each hand in a separate bowl of warm water.

Close your eyes and visualize roots sprouting from the base of your spine, burrowing deep into the earth. With each slow, deep inhalation, imagine these roots going deeper and deeper until they reach a bright, glowing light at the earth's core.

Now, envision two streams of light descending from the sky, one into each bowl. Feel the love of the God filling the bowl to your left, and the love of the Goddess filling the bowl to your right. Draw this divine love into your body through your hands, merging it with the earth's energy drawn up through your roots.

Focus on gathering all this powerful energy in your heart, where your most personal energy resides. Continue to build and concentrate this energy until you can contain it no more.

When you can no longer contain the energy in your heart, release it to flood your entire body. Shout aloud, "Heal me!" as you let the energy surge through you, spilling onto the ground and filling you with healing light.

Continue to draw energy for a while, letting it flow through your body and into the earth. Relax and bask in the peace and tranquility that follows.

After relaxing, draw your roots back into your body and remove your hands from the water. Sit up slowly.

Take a sip from the bowl to your left and thank the God for his love. Then, pour the remaining water at the base of a tree. Repeat this with the bowl to your right, thanking the Goddess for her love and pouring the water at the same tree.

In the future, care for this tree as a symbol of your connection to the healing energies you invoked.

NOTES

The Essential Book of Healing Spells and Magic

Elemental Healing Ritual

REQUIREMENTS:

❁ White clothing
❁ Elemental representation (choose based on ailment, e.g., stones for Earth, candles for Fire, incense for Air, dish of water for Water)
❁ Bucket of water (for fire safety)
❁ Cakes and wine (or bread and juice) for after-ritual meal

Element Correspondence:

Abdomen: Fire
Arms: Earth
Blood: Air
Bones: Earth
Chest: Air
Ears: Water
Eyes: Water
Feet: Earth
Genitalia: Fire
Hands: Earth
Heart: Fire
Legs: Earth
Lungs: Air
Mind: Fire
Nose: Air
Skin: Earth
Stomach: Water
Teeth: Earth
Throat: Air
Uterus: Water

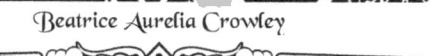

Instructions:

Begin by taking a ritual bath to cleanse and center yourself. Dress in all white clothing.

Create your sacred space and arrange the items representing your chosen element. If using Earth, gather stones or salt. For Fire, light candles. For Air, burn incense. For Water, place a dish of water or perform near a natural water source.

Cast your circle around the entire ritual area, invoking protection and sacredness.

Sit in the center with your element before you. Breathe deeply and slowly to reach a meditative state. Close your eyes and envision a pure white light enveloping you.

Hold the element in your hands. Feel its energy merging with yours. Say:

> "Element of [Element Name], hear my plea,
> Your healing power flows through me.
> Guide your strength to [Body Part], make it whole,
> Restore health and balance, body and soul."

Direct the energy of the element into the affected area. Visualize the ailment being healed. Continue until you feel a sense of peace and completion.

Thank the element and release it back to nature. Extinguish any candles carefully (pinch or use water). Close your circle by thanking each direction, starting from the North and moving clockwise.

Enjoy an after-ritual meal of cakes and wine, or bread and juice, to ground and complete the ritual.

Note: This ritual begins its healing work immediately, but allow time for the full effects. A minor ailment may take a week, while a major illness may take a month. If you are using medications or supplements, have them present during the ritual to charge them with magical energy, enhancing their effectiveness.

Enchanted Crystal Healing

REQUIREMENTS:

❈ 3 candles: 2 light blue, 1 white
❈ Equal parts Allspice & Rosemary or Healing incense
❈ Photo or paper with the recipient's name
❈ Small quartz crystal

INSTRUCTIONS:

Arrange your candles on your altar or workspace in a semi-circle, with the white candle between the two blue ones.

Place the incense burner above the white candle.

Place the photo or paper with the recipient's name in the center, and set the quartz crystal on top.

Light the incense, allowing its healing aroma to fill the space.

Light each candle, beginning with the white one and then the blue ones.

Center yourself, closing your eyes, and take deep breaths, inhaling the fragrant incense.

Visualize all ill health leaving the recipient and being replaced by healing light and energy.

As you gather your healing energy, say:

> "Candles of blue and purest white,
> Bring forth healing, banish the blight.
> Incense smoke, rise and clear,
> Dispel the sickness, bring good cheer."

When you feel ready, release your gathered energy, directing it through the quartz crystal and towards the recipient.

Allow the candles to burn for a while as you continue to focus on the recipient's healing.

Give the recipient the crystal to carry as a charm for continued good health.

NOTES

Enchanted Poppet Healing

REQUIREMENTS:

❋ A poppet (doll)
❋ Blessing oil
❋ Rosemary perfume oil
❋ Violet perfume oil
❋ Voodoo oil
❋ Damnation powder
❋ A piece of red cloth
❋ A small fire-safe container or cauldron

INSTRUCTIONS:

Sprinkle the poppet liberally with blessing oil.

Rub the perfume oils over your hands, blending their energies.

Hold your hands over the poppet's head, palms open, and chant:

> "By the powers that heal, so true,
> Recovery now comes to you.
> Heal and mend, pain be gone,
> Strength and health, return at dawn."

Blend equal amounts of Rosemary perfume oil, Violet perfume oil, Voodoo oil, and Damnation powder until it forms a paste.

Coat the doll from top to bottom with this mixture, infusing it with your healing intention.

As you anoint, repeat the healing chant:

> "By herbs and oils, combined with care,
> Health and strength fill the air.
> Heal and mend, pain be gone,
> Strength and health, return at dawn."

Carefully wrap the coated doll in the piece of red cloth.

Hide it away where it cannot be seen for several days, allowing the magic to work unseen.

After the designated days, take the doll to a safe place outdoors.

Burn it in a small fire-safe container or cauldron, scattering the ashes to the wind.

As you release the ashes, say:

> "As the flames consume,
> Illness be removed.
> As the ashes fly,
> Health and strength revive.
> Winds of the world, carry this plea,
> With this act, I set thee free."

NOTES

Empowering Healing Remedy

REQUIREMENTS:

- Green candle
- Herbs for burning: rosemary, juniper, lemon balm (or a preferred blend)
- Your healing potion or remedy

INSTRUCTIONS:

Cast your circle to create a sacred space. Light the green candle to represent healing and vitality.

Burn the chosen herbs (rosemary, juniper, lemon balm) or your preferred blend to fill the air with their essence.

Sit comfortably in the center of your circle, cross-legged or however you feel most at ease, facing north. If in the Southern Hemisphere, face south.

Place the healing remedy in your lap, cradling it between your palms.

If you are familiar with opening your chakras, do so now. Circulate the energies within your body, preparing to direct them into the remedy. If not, simply focus on channeling your healing intentions through your hands.

Visualize the person you are healing as completely well. Direct your healing energy into the potion, and chant:

"In the name of the great mother,
(Name) is completely well,
Health restored, all is swell."

Offer a final incense blessing to seal the energy. Close your chakras and the circle thoroughly, giving thanks for the healing energies.

Beatrice Aurelia Crowley

Eucalyptus Healing Spell

REQUIREMENTS:

✤ Three green candles
✤ Three Eucalyptus branches, leaves, or pods
✤ Essential oil (Eucalyptus, Peppermint, or Rosemary)

INSTRUCTIONS:

Arrange the three green candles in a circle. Place the Eucalyptus branches, leaves, or pods around the candles, creating a ring of healing energy.

Anoint each candle with a few drops of the chosen essential oil. As you do this, say:

*"With this oil, I consecrate,
Healing powers, activate."*

Stand before the candles, take a deep breath, and inhale the divine power. Visualize yourself enveloped in a soothing, green light, feeling completely healed and revitalized.

Light each candle, one by one, and as you do, chant:

*"By flame and leaf, I call to thee,
Healing powers, set me free.
Banish illness, pain, and strife,
Restore me now, grant me life."*

Sit quietly, inhaling the aromatic scent of Eucalyptus. Visualize the healing energy flowing through your body, especially focusing on areas of discomfort or illness. See the green light spreading, cleansing, and rejuvenating.

Allow the candles to burn down completely. As they do, feel the healing energy continue to work within you.

Once the candles are fully burned, gather the remaining Eucalyptus and place it near your bed or in a healing space to continue benefiting from its energy.

Flaming Image Healing

Requirements:

✿ Red Candle
✿ Drawing Paper
✿ Colored Pencils or Markers
✿ Heatproof Container

Instructions:

Draw a picture of yourself, clearly depicting the disease, wound, or condition.

Illustrate the problem vividly, such as a large hammer for a headache, black worms for a virus, or a broken limb.

Hold the red candle in your hands and close your eyes.

Focus on channeling healing energy into the candle, visualizing it glowing with vibrant, restorative light.

Light the red candle.

Hold the tip of the first drawing in the candle's flame until it catches fire.

Say:

*"Flame of healing, burn away,
All this pain and dark dismay."*

Drop the burning picture into a heatproof container, allowing it to turn to ash.

While the candle burns, draw a new picture of yourself completely healed and free from ailment.

Visualize yourself strong, healthy, and vibrant as you create the image.

Place the new, healed drawing under the red candle.

Say:

> "Candle's glow and healing might,
> Restore my health, day and night."

Let the candle burn down completely.

As the candle burns, close your eyes and focus on the healing light enveloping your entire being.

Feel the energy of the spell working through you, mending and restoring.

Once the candle has burned out, keep the healed drawing somewhere special as a reminder of the spell and the healing energy it has brought into your life.

NOTES

The Essential Book of Healing Spells and Magic

Gaia's Healing

REQUIREMENTS:

❈ Seashells (or stones, branches, and/or flowers if not at the beach)
❈ Blue candle
❈ Incense stick (any calming scent)

Timing: Perform this spell during an eclipse or when the Moon is waxing.

INSTRUCTIONS:

Find a secluded beach, forest, or garden.

Arrange the seashells (or alternative materials) to form a magic circle at least five feet in diameter.

Kneel in the center of the circle, facing the ocean (or a natural focal point if not by the sea).

Light the blue candle and the incense, placing them before you.

Raise your arms high with palms up in the traditional Witch's prayer position.

Recite the following chant:

> With smoke and flame, the spell ignites,
> O Goddess of stars, Moon's soft lights,
> Begin the healing, let it flow,
> Restore the Earth, make Her whole.
> The Earth, my Mother, I am Her child,
> She is my lover, untamed and wild.
> Heal Her surface, heal within,
> Land and sea, fire and wind.

With love sincere, I speak this plea,
To awaken care in humanity.
May sisters, brothers, near and far,
Heal the wounds of our Mother star.
Begin the healing, let it flow,
Restore the Earth, make Her whole.
Heal Her surface, heal within,
Land and sea, fire and wind.

Allow the incense to burn completely and the candle to burn down.

Reflect on the Earth's healing and your role in it.

Once the candle is extinguished, gather the materials and return them to their natural surroundings if possible.

NOTES

Heal a Friend or Relative

REQUIREMENTS:

- Purple paper
- White yarn or string
- Scissors
- Fresh violets (whole, with stems)
- Black pen
- Purple candle
- Small vase or holder (for flowers)

INSTRUCTIONS:

Light the purple candle, invoking healing energies.

Fill the small vase with water and place the freshly cut violets inside.

Hold the vase and say a chant, focusing on the well-being of your friend or relative:

> "Violets bright, in this light,
> Heal and strengthen with your might,
> Bring health anew, vibrant and true,
> Well-being blossom, whole and true."

Cut a heart shape from the purple paper.

On one side, write the person's name with the black pen.

On the other side, write a heartfelt "Get Well!" message.

Poke a small hole in the top right side of the heart.

Thread the white string through the hole, tying it securely.

Attach the enchanted heart to the vase.

Give the enchanted vase of violets to the person in need of healing.

Visualize their recovery as the violets radiate healing energy.

Heal All

REQUIREMENTS:

✦ Blue Candle
✦ Carving Tool (e.g., a pin or small knife)

INSTRUCTIONS:

Find a quiet and sacred space where you will not be disturbed.

Gather your materials and sit comfortably.

Take the blue candle and carve the name of the person in need of healing into the wax.

As you carve, focus your thoughts on the person's wellness and envision them in perfect health.

Light the blue candle, allowing its flame to illuminate the space.

Hold your hands over the candle, feeling its warmth and light.

Close your eyes and take a deep breath.

With intention and conviction, recite the spell:

> *"Healing light, shining bright,*
> *Chase away (Name)'s ailment in fright.*
> *With harm to none, including me,*
> *By my will, so shall it be."*

As the candle burns, visualize a radiant blue light enveloping the person, dissolving their sickness and filling them with vibrant health.

Imagine them smiling, strong, and full of energy.

Allow the candle to burn down completely, sealing the spell.

Sit in meditation, feeling the healing energy flow through you and toward the person in need.

Once the candle has burned out, trust that the healing energies have been set in motion.

Healing Bath Meditation

REQUIREMENTS:

✤ Silver or white candle
✤ Salt
✤ Healing oil (carnation, violet, sandalwood, or narcissus)

INSTRUCTIONS:

Light the silver or white candle to illuminate your bathroom. Let its gentle light fill the space, creating an aura of calm and healing.

Draw a tub of very warm water. As the tub fills, add a generous handful of salt to purify the water. Then, add a few drops of your chosen healing oil.

Step into the tub, allowing the warm, salted water to envelop you. Feel the water penetrating your skin, purging sickness from your body.

Close your eyes and visualize the 'black worms' of illness being drawn out of your body and into the water. See the sickness leaving your body and merging with the water.

When you feel ready, pull the plug and let the water drain away. As it does, chant:

> *The sickness is flowing out of me,*
> *Into the water, down to the sea.*

Only rise from the tub once it has completely drained. Rinse your body with fresh water (a shower works best) to cleanse away any remaining sickness.

Repeat this ritual as needed to accelerate your recovery and restore your health.

Healing Circle of Fire

REQUIREMENTS:

✤ Three purple candles
✤ Three blue candles
✤ A photograph of yourself

INSTRUCTIONS:

Place the candles in a circle around the photograph.

Charge each candle individually with the following incantation:

"By the powers of fire, East, South, West, and North;
By the powers of Earth, Air, Fire, and Water;
By the powers of the Sun, Moon, and Stars:
Heal me of this ailment, its causes and manifestations."

Light each candle and recite:

"Consume the sickness in your blaze,
Destroy the harm that it conveys.
With your strength, dispel the blight,
In your glow, restore my sight.
Free me from this pain and strife,
Banish all that hinders life.
Heal me now, set me free,
By my will, so let it be!"

The Essential Book of Healing Spells and Magic

Healing of the Seven Candles

REQUIREMENTS:

✵ Seven candles:
✵ One white candle for the Lady
✵ One yellow candle for the Lord
✵ One orange candle for encouragement and attraction
✵ One candle in your astral color (aura or preference)
✵ Three red candles for strength and health
✵ Light incense (optional)

INSTRUCTIONS:

Light the white candle for the Lady and the yellow candle for the Lord.

Light the incense if desired.

Sit quietly, envisioning goodness and health flowing into you.

Light the petitioner's candle (your astral color) and say:

"Health and vigor, to _____ I send,
Blessings from the divine to mend."

Light the orange candle and say:

"This flame attracts all good things to _____,
Bringing health, strength, and his/her dreams."

Light the three red candles, one by one, saying:

"Strength and health, three times three,
Fill _____ with vitality."

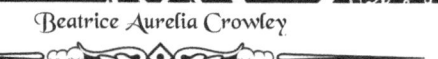

Sit and meditate on the good health you desire for the person.

Visualize the red candles' energy moving towards the petitioner's candle.

Extinguish the candles after meditation.

Repeat this ritual every day for seven days.

Each day, move the red candles closer to the petitioner's candle.

On the seventh Friday, let the red candles touch the petitioner's candle, and allow them to burn fully.

NOTES

Healing Ritual

REQUIREMENTS:

❋ Green Candle (for healing)
❋ Healing Oil
❋ Healing Incense

INSTRUCTIONS:

Anoint the green candle with the healing oil. As you do, visualize the person you wish to heal. See them in your mind's eye, happy and healthy.

Light the healing incense and let its aroma fill the space, creating an aura of healing and calm.

With the candle before you, focus your energy and chant:

Wrapped in cotton, bound by love,
Protected from pain, like a glove.
Brightest blessings surround tonight,
Cared for and healed by thoughts in flight.

Continue to visualize the person enveloped in a healing light, free from pain and full of vitality.

Allow the candle to burn down completely, releasing the healing energy into the universe.

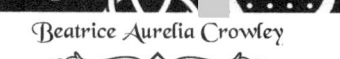

Hematite Healing

REQUIREMENTS:

✤ A Hematite stone

INSTRUCTIONS:

Sit in a quiet, comfortable place.

Hold the Hematite stone in your hand, feeling its cool surface and weight.

Close your eyes and focus on the vibrations of the Hematite stone.

Channel your healing energy into the stone, imagining it filling with vibrant light.

While holding the stone, chant with intent:

> "Stone of Hematite, gleaming dark,
> Grant me healing, ignite the spark.
> Hematite, with your power bright,
> Heal me swiftly, day and night."

Continue to hold the stone, envisioning it glowing with healing energy.

Feel the energy being absorbed by your body, bringing relief and wellness.

Keep the Hematite stone close to you, in a pocket or under your pillow, to maintain the healing connection.

No Ingredients Healing Chant

INSTRUCTIONS:

Place your hands gently over the wound.

Close your eyes and take a deep breath, centering your energy.

Rub the wound gently as you chant the following spell.

Chant:

> Blessed wound, in sacred time,
> By the Goddess' power, pure and fine.
> Mysteries of women, strong and bright,
> Heal this wound with song and light.

For a male witch, simply adjust the words to align with male energies and invoke the power of the God.

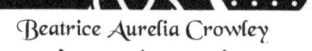

Protect and Maintain Good Health

REQUIREMENTS:

- 1 red candle
- 1 black candle
- 1 green candle

INSTRUCTIONS:

Find a quiet, sacred space to perform the spell.
Place the candles in a triangular formation on your altar.
Light the red candle first and say:

"I invoke Gangida, great protector,
May we guard your treasures, our bodies, forever."

Light the black candle and recite:

"Nullify disease as it draws near,
Arm my blood with guards, and banish all fear."

Light the green candle and chant:

"Gangida, grant protection from all that may harm,
From heavens above, to earth's strong arm.
Shield me from east to south, from west to north,
Keep my body healthy, let wellness come forth."

Stand before the candles, feeling their combined energies surrounding you.
Visualize a radiant light encasing your body, filling you with health and vitality.
Hold this vision and gratitude for a few moments before extinguishing the candles in reverse order.

Protect Against Disease

REQUIREMENTS:

✤ A small vial of volcanic ash (symbolic, can be substituted with a small stone if volcanic ash is not available)
✤ A red candle (for the fiery volcanoes)
✤ A white candle (for purity and protection)
✤ Incense of sage or rosemary (for purification)
✤ A bowl of spring water (for the essence of earth and sky)

INSTRUCTIONS:

Light the white candle to invite purity and protection into your space.

Light the red candle to symbolize the fiery volcanoes.

Burn the sage or rosemary incense to purify the air around you.

Hold the vial of volcanic ash or the stone in your hands.

Close your eyes and focus on the power of the earth, sky, and fire.

Gaze into the flame of the red candle and say:

> Hail to the sky, vast and grand,
> Hail to the earth, steadfast land,
> Hail to volcanoes, with flames so bright,
> Burn away illness, with your might.
> Mighty spirits, hear my plea,
> Shield me from sickness, set me free!

Dip the volcanic ash or stone into the bowl of spring water, then place it near the burning candles.

Let the candles burn down completely, visualizing a shield of protection forming around you.

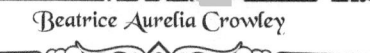

When the candles have burned down, sprinkle a few drops of the spring water around your space to seal the protection.

Keep the vial of volcanic ash or the stone with you as a protective talisman against disease.

NOTES

Salt Burial to Heal Another Person

REQUIREMENTS:

✣ Green candle
✣ Paper
✣ Bowl of salt
✣ Healing oil (optional)

INSTRUCTIONS:

Anoint the green candle with healing oil, if desired.

Light the candle.

Chant the afflicted person's name 10 times, invoking the divine or your chosen deity to heal them.

Recite:

> "Heal now, [Name], and bring them cheer,
> Illness be gone, let joy draw near,
> May health and happiness forever adhere."

Snuff out the candle.

Write the person's name on a sheet of paper.

Bury the paper in a bowl of salt to seal the healing spell.

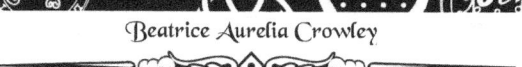

Beatrice Aurelia Crowley

Shower Waterfall of Healing

REQUIREMENTS:

✤ Shower with running water
✤ Towel for drying

INSTRUCTIONS:

Stand under the shower, close your eyes, and begin to visualize a powerful, serene waterfall cascading over you.

Speak these words aloud or in your mind:

> "Spirits of Water, pure and true,
> Cleanse my body, mind, and spirit anew.
> With healing power, consecrate me,
> Set me free, and let negativity flee."

As the water runs down your body, imagine all negativity, stress, and ailments swirling away and down the drain, leaving you purified and refreshed.

When you step out and begin to towel dry, chant:

> "Spirits of Air, swift and bright,
> Cleanse my body, mind, and spirit with light.
> Consecrate me, empower me strong,
> With healing winds, where I belong."

As you finish drying, envision yourself surrounded by a bright, healing aura, feeling completely rejuvenated and free from all negative energies.

The Essential Book of Healing Spells and Magic

Silver Moon Healing Charm

Requirements:

- A black candle
- A white candle
- Lavender oil
- Small silver charm (such as a moon or star)

Instructions:

Place the black candle on the left side and the white candle on the right. Anoint both candles with lavender oil, infusing them with your intent for healing and protection.

Cast a sacred circle to create a protected space for your ritual.

Light the black candle first, representing the waning moon, and say:

> "With each dark and passing night,
> As the moon doth wane from sight,
> Keep me in the Lady's care,
> Take this pain, lift it to air."

Hold the silver charm and anoint it with lavender oil. As you do this, say:

> "Banish all that wish me harm,
> Keep me well within your charm,
> May your blessings shield from ill,
> Hide me from another's will."

Light the white candle, representing the waxing moon, and say:

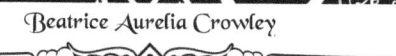

> "As the moon returns to round,
> Waxing fuller, strong, and sound,
> May my health and strength rebound,
> With your grace, keep me unbound."

Allow the candles to burn down completely if safe to do so. Close your circle, thanking the Lady for her protection and healing.

Carry the silver charm with you as a talisman of ongoing protection and healing.

NOTES

Stream Healing Ritual

REQUIREMENTS:

✤ A clean and quiet stream

INSTRUCTIONS:

Find a serene, clean stream where you can feel at peace.

Remove your clothes and step into the stream, immersing your entire body if possible.

Stand or lie in the stream, feeling the water envelop you.

Visualize the water flowing through and around you, cleansing away all illness and disease.

With the vision of the water drawing out the sickness, chant the following words:

> This sickness flows, it must depart,
> From my body, heart to heart.
> Into the river, let it be,
> Down to the sea, I am set free.

Once you feel the healing is complete, step out of the water and dry yourself.

Embrace the refreshed and purified feeling, knowing the spell is complete.

Concoctions

Balm of Gilead Salve

For inflammation and superficial skin conditions such as psoriasis, eczema, sunburn, rashes, insect bites and chapped skin.

REQUIREMENTS:

- 1 oz Balm of Gilead buds
- 1 pint hot olive oil
- 1.5 oz beeswax
- 0.5 tsp tincture of benzoin

INSTRUCTIONS:

Place the Balm of Gilead buds into a cauldron and pour the hot olive oil over them. Let the magical brew simmer, covered, for 3 hours. This allows the healing essence to infuse into the oil.

Strain the mixture carefully to remove the buds, retaining the now-enchanted oil.

Return the strained oil to the cauldron. Add the beeswax, stirring until it melts completely. Then, incorporate the tincture of benzoin to preserve your sacred salve.

Test the consistency by placing a small amount on a cool surface. Adjust with more beeswax for firmness or more oil for softness, if needed.

Pour the warm, enchanted salve into sterile jars. Allow it to cool and solidify, ready to be used for healing.

Chant:

> "Balm of Gilead, buds so rare,
> In olive oil, your powers share.
> With beeswax firm and benzoin pure,
> Craft a salve to heal and cure.
> For burns and wounds,
> your touch will mend,
> With magic's might,
> let pain descend."

NOTES

Bath Water

REQUIREMENTS:

❊ 10 drops olive oil
❊ 10 drops cypress oil
❊ 10 drops lavender oil
❊ Sandalwood oil (for anointing)
❊ Yellow and blue candles

INSTRUCTIONS:

Add 10 drops each of olive oil, cypress oil, and lavender oil to your bath water.

Anoint your hand with sandalwood oil.

Skim your hand over the surface of the water 3 to 12 times while chanting:

*"Within this water, power flows,
Stress unwinds, and healing grows."*

Light the yellow and blue candles.

Enter the tub and soak, allowing the vapors to take away your stress and hurts.

Healing Honey Remedies

Daily Health

REQUIREMENTS:

- Local raw honey
- Fresh ginger root
- Fresh lemon
- Cayenne pepper
- Fresh garlic cloves
- Cheesecloth (optional)
- Clean bandages (for wound dressing)

Advice on Honey:

For medicinal use, always choose honey from a local apiary. Consuming local pollens found in honey can enhance resistance to allergies over time. Ensure the honey is raw, unheated, and unprocessed to retain its magical healing properties.

Honey Flu Remedy

REQUIREMENTS:

❈ Six-inch ginger root
❈ 3 cups fresh water
❈ Juice of half a lemon
❈ Pinch of cayenne pepper
❈ Honey to taste

INSTRUCTIONS:

Slice the ginger root and place it in a non-aluminum pot with fresh water.

Cover the pot and bring to a gentle simmer, letting it cook for about twenty minutes.

Remove from heat, add lemon juice, cayenne pepper, and honey to taste.

This enchanted brew is ideal for soothing bronchitis and flu.

Honey Throat Syrup

REQUIREMENTS:

❈ Several cloves of fresh garlic
❈ Juice of half a lemon
❈ 1 cup raw honey

INSTRUCTIONS:

Blend the garlic cloves with lemon juice until smooth.

Add raw honey and blend again until well mixed.

Take in teaspoon doses for a sore throat, or strain through cheesecloth and bottle for future use.

Beatrice Aurelia Crowley

Garlic and Honey Wound Dressing

REQUIREMENTS:

- Fresh garlic (chopped or mashed)
- Raw honey
- Clean bandages

INSTRUCTIONS:

Carefully wash the cut or wound.

Apply chopped or mashed garlic to kill bacteria or viruses.

Cover the garlic with a generous layer of honey.

Secure with a clean bandage. The honey's anaerobic properties will prevent bacteria growth.

Healing Oil

Use the enchanted healing oil as needed by anointing the affected area of the body, adding a few drops to a warm bath, or using it in a diffuser to fill your space with its restorative fragrance.

Store the oil in a cool, dark place to maintain its potency.

REQUIREMENTS:

- 1/2 oz of base oil (choose from jojoba, almond, grapeseed, etc.)
- 5 drops Lavender oil
- 5 drops Camphor oil
- 5 drops Eucalyptus oil
- 5 drops Orange oil
- 3 drops Rosemary oil
- 2 drops Pine oil
- 4 drops Sandalwood oil

INSTRUCTIONS:

Pour the base oil into the glass bottle, taking a moment to center yourself and focus on the healing energy you wish to infuse into the oil.

Add each essential oil one by one, starting with Lavender oil and ending with Sandalwood oil. As you add each drop, visualize the specific healing properties it brings into the blend.

Once all the oils are combined, hold the bottle between your hands, close your eyes, and take several deep breaths.

Chant the following incantation to charge the oil with your intent

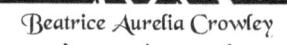

Beatrice Aurelia Crowley

Oils of healing, pure and bright,
Blend your magic, day and night.
With lavender's calm and camphor's might,
Eucalyptus clear and orange light.
Rosemary's strength, pine's ancient call,
Sandalwood's peace, combine them all.
By my will, this oil is blessed,
To bring good health and peaceful rest.

NOTES

Healing Potpourri I

REQUIREMENTS:

✣ 1 part rosemary
✣ 1 part juniper berries, bruised to release the smell

INSTRUCTIONS:

Mix rosemary and bruised juniper berries together.

Place the blend in a small sachet or bowl.

Set it in a room where healing energies are needed, allowing the aroma to fill the space with restorative power.

Healing Potpourri II

REQUIREMENTS:

- ❂ 2 parts myrrh
- ❂ 1 part cinnamon
- ❂ 1 pinch saffron

INSTRUCTIONS:

Combine myrrh, cinnamon, and saffron in a bowl.

Place the mixture in a sachet or decorative dish.

Position it in an area where you seek healing, letting the fragrant blend enhance the environment with its magical properties.

The Essential Book of Healing Spells and Magic

Healing Potpourri III

Requirements:

✵ 3 parts myrrh
✵ 2 parts nutmeg
✵ 1 part cedar
✵ 1 part clove
✵ 1/2 part lemon balm
✵ 1/2 part pine needles or sap

Instructions:

Mix all the ingredients thoroughly in a bowl.

Transfer the blend to a sachet or potpourri dish.

Place it in your home, allowing the enchanting scent to promote healing and well-being throughout the space.

Beatrice Aurelia Crowley

Healing Tea

REQUIREMENTS:

✤ 1 tablespoon China black tea
✤ 2 teaspoons fennel
✤ 1 teaspoon mint
✤ 2 teaspoons rose hips
✤ 1 teaspoon elder flower
✤ 2 teaspoons hops
✤ 1 teaspoon mullein

INSTRUCTIONS:

Blend all ingredients together in a bowl.

Boil water and pour over **1** teaspoon of the tea blend per cup.

Steep for **5-7** minutes.

Strain and enjoy, envisioning health and vitality flowing into your body with each sip.

Irish Healing Water

Anoint the spots where illness lurks, or if unsure where the discomfort lies, anoint your belly. Alternatively, pour the contents into your bath water for a healing soak.

REQUIREMENTS:

- Equal parts of lavender, violet, and rosemary
- One quart of water
- A jar
- A coffee filter

INSTRUCTIONS:

Begin by taking equal parts of lavender, violet, and rosemary. Empower them with your intention for healing.

Boil the empowered herbs in a pot with about a quart of water over medium heat. Allow the water to become richly colored and the herbs to fill your kitchen with their scent.

Strain the water into a jar using a coffee filter to remove all herbal residues.

Place the jar in sunlight for an entire day to absorb the radiant energies of the sun. For additional potency, perform this on a Wednesday to harness the healing powers of Mercury.

Occasionally, look at the jar and add your own healing energies to it throughout the day.

Just before sundown, fetch the jar and hold it firmly between your hands, just below your navel. Focus your desire to be well, filling the jar with this intention. Visualize it glowing brightly, infused with the sun's energy.

Chant these words until the jar is filled with as much energy as it can hold:

> "By the herb and by the sun,
> Wellness and I are now as one.
> Strengthening energies now are merged,
> Baneful energies now be purged."

NOTES

Jewelweed Salve

Because of its antipruritic qualities, it is most frequently used topically to treat poison ivy rash. Additionally, it is used to treat bruising and swelling, increase blood flow, and reduce joint and postpartum pain.

REQUIREMENTS:

- 2 ounces dried Jewelweed herb (or 4 ounces fresh)
- 2 cups vegetable oil (olive, almond, sesame, or soy)
- 1/4 tsp Vitamin E oil or Tincture of Benzoin (for preservation, if storing)
- 1 Tbsp beeswax or paraffin

INSTRUCTIONS:

Combine Jewelweed herb and vegetable oil in a double boiler.

Simmer on low heat for 1 to 2 hours, allowing the herb's essence to infuse the oil.

Strain the mixture into a sterilized jar. If not using immediately, add Vitamin E oil or Tincture of Benzoin for preservation.

Gently heat 4 ounces of the infused oil in the top of a double boiler.

Add 1 Tbsp of beeswax or paraffin to the warmed oil.

Let the beeswax or paraffin melt completely, stirring to combine.

Add 1/8 to 1/4 teaspoon Vitamin E oil or Tincture of Benzoin to preserve the salve.

Mix well, then pour or spoon the mixture into a jar.

Allow the salve to cool and then cap the jar.

As you prepare your salve, you may wish to recite:

"Herbs of green, heal and mend,
Oil of life, your strength I blend.
Wax of bees, bind and hold,
Salve of magic, cure and bold."
Let the salve cool, then seal the jar.

NOTES

Menopause Elixir

Use the elixir as needed to bring balance and ease to your body, taking it with reverence and gratitude for the natural wisdom of the herbs.

REQUIREMENTS:

- 1 part Chasteberry
- 1 part Dong Quai
- 1 part Wild Yam Root
- 1/2 part Hops
- 1/2 part Valerian
- 1/2 part Passionflower
- 1/2 part Dandelion Root
- 1/2 part Uva-ursi
- 1/2 part Cornsilk
- 1/2 part Juniper berries
- 50% alcohol (enough to cover the herbs)

INSTRUCTIONS:

At the rise of a new moon, gather the sacred herbs and place them in a glass jar. As you do so, whisper your intention for balance and harmony during this transitional phase of life.

Cover the herbs with 50% alcohol, ensuring they are fully submerged. Seal the jar tightly and shake it gently, envisioning the healing energies of the herbs merging with the liquid.

For the next six weeks, shake the jar daily. Each time you shake it, chant:

> "Herbs of power, blend and weave,
> Balance and calm, may I receive.
> By moon and star, and earth so true,
> Heal my body, through and through."

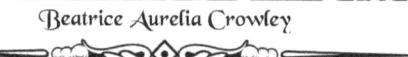

After six weeks, strain the mixture to remove the herbs, keeping only the enchanted liquid. Store this magical elixir in a dark, cool place, within a vessel that feels sacred to you.

NOTES

Muscle Pain Reliever

REQUIREMENTS:

- 1 tablespoon cayenne powder
- 1 tablespoon wormwood
- 1 tablespoon tansy flower
- 8 ounces vinegar
- 1/2 ounce spirits of camphor
- 8 ounces turpentine
- Cheesecloth for straining

INSTRUCTIONS:

Combine the cayenne powder, wormwood, and tansy flower in a cauldron or pot.

Gently warm the mixture with the vinegar, stirring to dissolve the powders.

Allow the mixture to cool and then strain it through cheesecloth into a clean container.

Add the spirits of camphor and turpentine to the herbal vinegar mixture.

Stir the concoction clockwise, envisioning it filled with potent healing energy.

Hold your hands over the mixture and chant:

> "By herbs and fire, this potion blend,
> Muscle pain and aches now mend.
> Blood shall flow with vigor anew,
> Health and strength return to you."

Application:

Use this powerful liniment to massage the affected areas.

Feel the warmth and energy spreading through your skin, easing the pain and restoring comfort.

Note: This liniment is potent due to its rubefacient properties, stimulating blood flow to the surface of the skin to relieve muscle pain.

NOTES

Moon Water Tonic

Drink this enchanted moon water every morning to align your body, mind, and spirit, preparing yourself for the day ahead.

REQUIREMENTS:

✤ Clear quartz crystal
✤ Clear glass
✤ 1 cup purified water
✤ Clear plastic wrap

Timing:

Check an almanac for the exact time of sundown on your chosen day.

INSTRUCTIONS:

Wait for a clear night, ideally on or just before the full moon.

Place the clear quartz crystal in the clear glass.

Fill the glass with one cup of purified water.

At sundown, place the glass outdoors in a spot where it will be bathed in moonlight.

Cover the glass with clear plastic wrap to keep it pure.

At dawn, remove the glass. The water is now charged with lunar energy.

Chant:

*Moon so bright, grant your light,
Infuse this water with your might.
Healing power, pure and true,
Bring balance to body, mind, and soul anew.*

Rejuvenating Bath

This bath will relieve sinus issues, ease cold symptoms, boost metabolism, and soothe muscular pain.

Ingredients:

- 1/2 cup yarrow flowers
- 1/2 cup elder flowers
- 1/2 cup mint leaves
- 1/2 cup rose petals

Instructions:

Place the herbs in a cheesecloth or nylon bundle.

Let the bundle steep in your bath for a few minutes.

Use the bundle to gently scrub your body as you relax in the bath.

Prepare a hot infusion of chamomile, yarrow flowers, elder flowers, and mint leaves to drink while you bathe.

Chant:

As herbs and petals blend with the steam,
Sinus relief and cold's end I dream.
Metabolism and muscles feel the might,
In this bath, all becomes right.

The Essential Book of Healing Spells and Magic

Pain Reliever Salve

REQUIREMENTS:

❋ 1 oz chickweed (for reducing inflammation and aiding in healing)
❋ 1 oz wormwood (a potent pain reliever)
❋ 1 oz yarrow (an anti-bacterial agent that also helps relieve pain and stops bleeding)
❋ 2 pints olive oil
❋ 3 oz beeswax
❋ 1 tsp tincture of benzoin

INSTRUCTIONS:

Mix together 1 oz of chickweed, 1 oz of wormwood, and 1 oz of yarrow in a bowl. As you combine the herbs, chant:

*"Chickweed for healing, so gentle and kind,
Wormwood for pain, relief I shall find,
Yarrow to cleanse and to heal wounds anew,
Together in this oil, their magic imbue."*

Add the herbal mixture to 2 pints of olive oil in a double boiler. Simmer gently for 3 hours, stirring occasionally. As the herbs infuse, visualize their healing properties merging with the oil.

After 3 hours, strain the oil into a sterilized bowl, removing all the herb remnants. Return the oil to the double boiler and add 3 oz of beeswax. Allow the beeswax to melt completely, stirring gently. As you stir, say:

*"Wax of the bees, solid and pure,
Combine with this oil to heal and to cure."*

Add 1 teaspoon of tincture of benzoin to the mixture for preservation. Stir well, chanting:

> "Benzoin for strength, protection, and might,
> Preserve this salve, from morning to night."

Test the salve for consistency by placing a small amount on a cool surface. Adjust the beeswax if needed. Once satisfied, pour the warm salve into wide-mouth containers. Allow to cool and solidify.

Once cooled, hold your hands over the containers and visualize a healing light enveloping them. Say:

> "By earth and sky, by moon and sun,
> Pain be banished, healing begun.
> This salve I empower with magic divine,
> To heal and soothe, to be a sign."

Soothing Bath

This bath soothes the skin and enhances circulation.

INGREDIENTS:

- 1/2 cup comfrey leaves
- 1/2 cup chamomile flowers
- 1/2 cup lavender flowers
- 1/2 cup mint leaves

INSTRUCTIONS:

Place the herbs in a cheesecloth or nylon bundle.

Let the bundle steep in your bath for a few minutes, just as for the rejuvenating bath.

Relax and feel the soothing effects.

Chant:

> Leaves and blooms, within the water's flow,
> Soothe my skin, let circulation grow.
> Lavender, chamomile, mint, and comfrey,
> Bless my bath, set my spirit free.

Books by this Author

- The Protection Bible - The Essential Book of Protection Spells and Magic
- The Essential Book of Binding Spells and Magic
- The Essential Book of Cleansing, Blessing, and Purification Spells and Magic
- The Essential Book of Glamour and Beauty Spells and Magic
- The Essential Book of Healing Spells and Magic
- The Essential Book of Household Spells and Magic
- The Essential Book of Love Spells and Magic

More Books by Erebus Society

The Standard Book of Candle Magic
by K.P. Theodore

In The Standard Book of Candle Magic you will learn about the use of candles in magical traditions, the meanings of colours so you can create your own candle magic rituals, how to prepare for magical practice, how to cast a standard circle, and over 30 Candle Magic spells for your everyday magical needs.

The Standard Book of Meditation
by K.P. Theodore

Within the pages of this book, you will find a diverse array of meditation techniques waiting to be explored. From breath awareness to body scan, loving-kindness to visualization, the author has meticulously assembled a rich tapestry of practices that invite you to embark on a transformative inner journey.

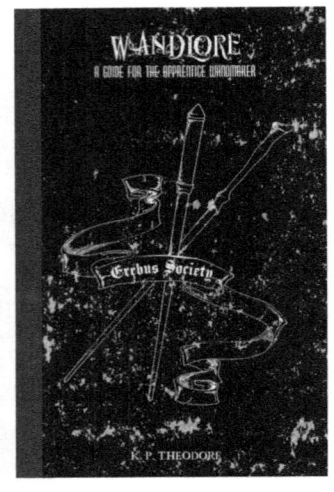

Wandlore - A Guide for the Apprentice Wandmaker

by K.P. Theodore

Delve into the ancient and intricate art of wandmaking with this comprehensive guide to the origins, properties, and crafting of magick wands. This book serves as both an introduction to wandlore and a hands-on manual for those who aspire to become skilled wand makers.

The Magic of Armadel - A 17th Century Grimoire in Full Colour

by Victor Shaw

The Grimoire of Armadel is a book of Celestial Magick and contains information, seals, and sigils of Angels, Demons and other Celestial Spirits.

It is classed as a Christian/Theistic Grimoire, and it was first translated by S.L. McGregor Mathers in the late 1890's from the original French and Latin manuscript that can be found in the Biblotheque l'Arsenal in Paris.

The Grimoire of Ceremonial Magick

by Victor Shaw

This book is a collection of passages, rites, practices, and rituals from various famous Grimoires. It is a cluster of the most obscure and powerful invocations, ceremonies, and pacts, and it explains their history and origins while it refutes certain myths surrounding Ancient Grimoires, and discusses the theology therein.

The Ripley Scroll: A Facsimile of the Pursuit for the Philosopher's Stone

by Victor Shaw

The 'Ripley scroll' or 'Ripley Scrowle' is a paramount alchemical work of the 15th century as it depicts the mystical and laborious process for the pursuit of the Philosopher's Stone. A legendary substance that can turn base metals into gold and can also be used in the making of the elixir of life, providing its possessor with prolonged life or even Immortality.

The Fundamental Book of Sigil Magick

by K.P. Theodore

This book serves as a textbook for those who wish to study the art of Sigil Magick. In its pages you will find information about the different kinds of sigils, their use, activation techniques and how to create custom tailored sigils from scratch.

Learn how to captivate emotions, empower the mind, create mental barriers, re-program the brain and alter consciousness by the use of "Mental Sigils".

The Accelerated Necromancer

by Gavin Fox

Necromancy has long been misunderstood, reduced to taboo and superstition. In this insightful work, Gavin redefines the practice, blending witchcraft and chaos magick to offer a responsible, spiritually enriching path.

With practical techniques, seasonal rites, and a fresh take on working with the dead, this book is a must-read for those seeking to walk the shadows with wisdom and reverence.

www.ingramcontent.com/pod-product-compliance
Lightning Source LLC
Chambersburg PA
CBHW020016050426
42450CB00005B/493